ENGLISH HOUSES

by

BRUCE MUNRO

(Fellow of the Incorporated Society of Valuers and Auctioneers)

THE ESTATES GAZETTE LIMITED

151 WARDOUR STREET LONDON W1V 4BN

Designed by David Stock and Associates, printed by photo lithography
and bound in Great Britain at the Pitman Press, Bath

ENGLISH HOUSES

INTRODUCTION

These notes have been prepared principally for those whose occupation is the sale of houses: Estate Agents, Auctioneers and Surveyors. They may also interest others involved in buying, selling, building (and even living in) houses.

They are intended to help readers, quickly and **quite superficially**, improve their knowledge of domestic architecture.

Houses reveal the taste of those who built, owned and lived in them.

Over the centuries different generations have created different styles, all with their own particular features.

As time has passed, succeeding generations have altered original buildings to such an extent that a large proportion of houses in this country are a hotchpotch of many periods. Even the original buildings which seem "of a piece" may have been built in several stages.

In this little book the salient external architectural features are described, and the illustrated glossary should cover most things not shown in the photographs.

Not every style of house is covered by the illustrations but they do give a lead to many and may encourage the reader to enquire more thoroughly into the date of a building and so describe more factually and carefully its features.

Many of the illustrations show houses of early date refaced in later centuries and it should be borne in mind that a very late and ordinary looking house may sometimes conceal internal features of great age and interest.

The examples here are from North Essex and East Anglia and therefore show the materials used in those areas but the design features are generally common to all Britain.

THE PERIODS

The dates of the periods are not hard and fast, and vary in different publications.
Within reason the following are usually accepted:–

		THE SOVEREIGN	
TUDOR 1485-1560	*Henry VII*	*1485-1509*
	Henry VIII	*1509-1547*
	Edward VI	*1547-1553*
	Mary	*1553-1558*
ELIZABETHAN 1560-1603	*Elizabeth I*	*1558-1603*
JACOBEAN or	*James I*	*1603-1625*
EARLY STUART 1603-1649	*Charles I*	*1625-1649*
CROMWELLIAN 1649-1660	*Commonwealth*	
CAROLEAN or	*Charles II*	*1660-1685*
LATE STUART 1660-1689	*James II*	*1685-1689*
WILLIAM &	*William III*	
MARY 1689-1702	*and Mary*	*1689-1702*

		THE SOVEREIGN	
QUEEN ANNE 1702-1714	*Anne*	*1702-1714*
GEORGIAN 1714-1800	*George I*	*1714-1727*
	George II	*1727-1760*
	George III	*1760-1820*
REGENCY and	*George III*	
EARLY VICTORIAN .1800-1837	*George IV*	*1820-1830*
	William IV	*1830-1837*
VICTORIAN 1837-1901	*Victoria*	*1837-1901*
EDWARDIAN 1901-1910	*Edward VII*	*1901-1910*

The Medieval period is taken to end at the Battle of Bosworth in 1485. It is not included in the table above, but the origins of many houses date from the 15th century and before.

THE ORDERS

The architecture of ancient Greece and Rome is known as Classical Architecture. The forms and decorations were revived in Italy in the 15th and 16th centuries and were fashionable in Britain from the late 16th century onwards.

The columns evolved by the Greeks and Romans together with the lintels over them are called the "Orders" and have greatly influenced British architecture.

Many of the doorcases of houses since the seventeenth century are based on these orders.

Here are the three main types of orders consisting of columns with their capitals and bases.

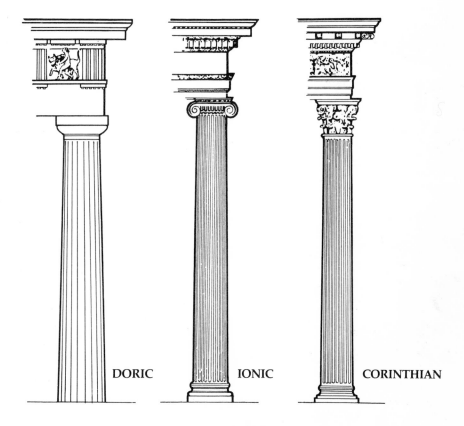

DORIC   IONIC   CORINTHIAN

THE ARCHES

The shapes of the arches above windows and doors
are referred to as follows:–

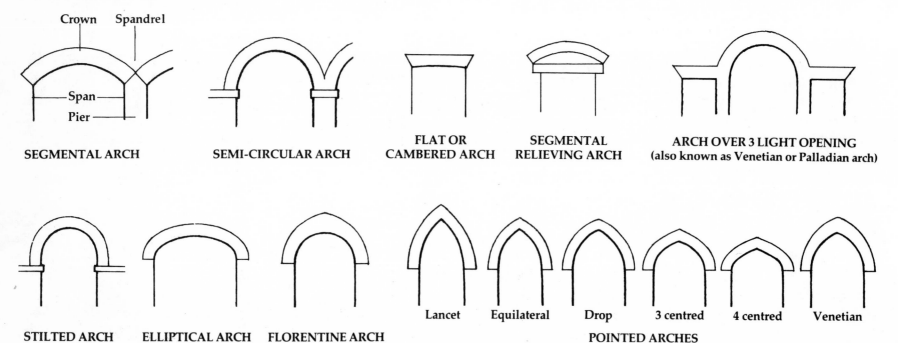

SEGMENTAL ARCH **SEMI-CIRCULAR ARCH** **FLAT OR CAMBERED ARCH** **SEGMENTAL RELIEVING ARCH** **ARCH OVER 3 LIGHT OPENING** (also known as Venetian or Palladian arch)

STILTED ARCH **ELLIPTICAL ARCH** **FLORENTINE ARCH** Lancet Equilateral Drop 3 centred 4 centred Venetian **POINTED ARCHES**

THE ROOFS

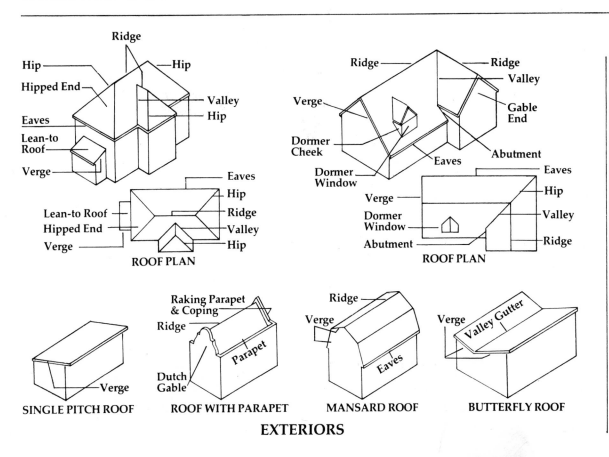

Ridge

Hip

Hipped End

Eaves

Lean-to Roof

Verge

Hip

Valley

Hip

Eaves

Lean-to Roof

Hipped End

Verge

Eaves

Hip

Ridge

Valley

Hip

ROOF PLAN

Ridge

Verge

Dormer Cheek

Dormer Window

Ridge

Valley

Gable End

Abutment

Eaves

Verge

Dormer Window

Abutment

Eaves

Hip

Valley

Ridge

ROOF PLAN

Verge

SINGLE PITCH ROOF

Raking Parapet & Coping

Ridge

Parapet

Dutch Gable

ROOF WITH PARAPET

Ridge

Verge

Eaves

MANSARD ROOF

Verge

Valley Gutter

BUTTERFLY ROOF

EXTERIORS

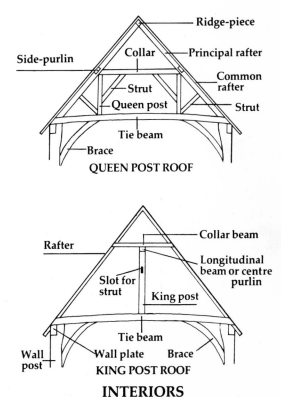

Side-purlin

Ridge-piece

Collar

Principal rafter

Common rafter

Strut

Queen post

Strut

Tie beam

Brace

QUEEN POST ROOF

Rafter

Collar beam

Slot for strut

Longitudinal beam or centre purlin

King post

Tie beam

Wall post

Wall plate

Brace

KING POST ROOF

INTERIORS

5

BUILDING MATERIALS

Main walls

The type of building materials used for the walls depends upon the type of construction.

The two structural systems for houses are:–

1. Solid construction in which the loads of roof and floors are carried to foundation by walls.

2. Frame construction in which the loads of roof and floors are carried by a timber frame which in turn is covered for weather protection.

In the former system, the materials used include solid forms, for example brick, flint, and in the latter the frame which is of timber has a protective covering or infill of wattle and daub, lath and plaster, brick nogging or weatherboard.

The principal building materials are as follows:–

Ashlar

Hewn stone, used for facing to give a high quality finish.

Brick

The universal building material in England and Wales by mid Victorian times. The pattern in which the bricks are laid is referred to as BONDING.

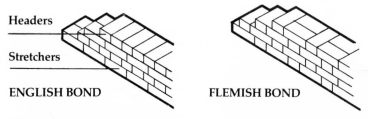

Bricks have varied in size through the centuries. Here is a guide to their dates:

GREAT BRICKS	1200-1520	12″ × 6″ × 1¾″ to 2¾″
FLEMISH BRICKS	13th C-1571	8″ to 9¾″ × 3¾″ to 4¾″ × 1¾″ to 2½″
STATUTE BRICKS (regulated by law)	1571	9″×4½″×2½″
MODERN BRICKS	18th C	8½″×4″×2¼″ 8¾″×4″×2⅝″ or 2⅞″

Individual kilns (for example on landed estates) had their own peculiar dimensions.

BUILDING MATERIALS

Brick nogging
Brick filling, sometimes in herringbone pattern, in between timber studs.

Cob
Mud mixed with water and wheat straw, then plastered over.

Clay bat
Clay mixed with straw and shaped in rectangular blocks.

Clunch
The usual name for chalk blocks.

Cobblestones
Rounded stones picked from river beds or fields, usually used on small dwellings.

Flint
Flints picked from the fields are irregular in shape and the exposed ends in a wall are often round topped. If knapped they are square topped and smooth.

Half timber
Timber framework usually oak, with the spaces in between the vertical studs filled with (1) plaster on wooden laths or (2) wattle and daub, a form of similar infilling in which clay, dung, horsehair etc. was daubed onto interwoven wattles. Often the whole was plastered over and patterned. The patterning is called pargetting or pargework.

Stone
Stone from the fields or quarry, depending on the particular area of the country, was used for main walls.

Stucco
A form of cement used to cover brick or stone.

Vertical tiles or slates
Tiles or slates hung on laths (also called hanging tiles or slates).

Weatherboarding (or clapboard)
Long timber horizontal boards nailed to the framework and tarred or painted.

ROOFING MATERIALS

Thatch
the principal thatching materials are straw and reed.
Wheat straw is most common. Reed is specially
grown in Norfolk.

Slate
Slate comes from quarries mainly in Wales, the West
Country and the Lake District.
It began to come into use throughout the country in
the late 18th century.
Welsh Slate is used in thin slabs of uniform thickness
and size. Other slates are more irregular.

Stone Tiles are quarried and are to be found in the
North and West of the country.

Plain Tiles
Clay tiles 10½"×6½"×½" were standardised in 1477
and are still manufactured in this size.
Tiles are laid on battens originally held in position by
wooden pegs (peg tiles) and later by nibs moulded in
the tile. Modern tiles are of concrete.

Pan Tiles
Shaped tiles moulded in an "S" curve which, when
laid, slightly overlap each other vertically.

Cedar Shingles
Rectangular cedar wood tiles.

Asbestos Tiles
Rectangular asbestos tiles.

(Modern roofing materials include layers of
bituminous felt and ashphalt on flat roofs.)

GLOSSARY

Architrave
A moulded enrichment to the jambs and head of a doorway or window opening.

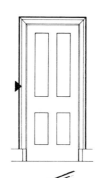

Baluster
A post supporting a hand rail, usually part of a series called a balustrade.

Barge-board
A board, sometimes carved, fixed to the edge of a gabled roof, a short distance from the face of the walls.

Bay Window
Projecting windows with angles.

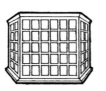

Bow Window
Projecting convex window.

Brace
In roof construction, a timber inserted to strengthen the framing of a truss.

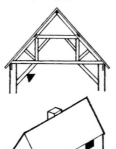

Bressumer
A beam forming the direct support of an upper wall in timber framing, similar to a lintel.

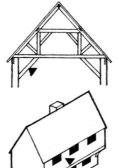

Buttress
Projecting masonry built against a wall to give additional strength.

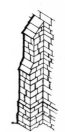

Canopy
A projection or hood over a door or window.

Casement
The hinged part of a window.

Collar-beam
A horizontal beam serving to tie a pair of rafters together some distance above the wall plate level.

GLOSSARY

Corbel
A projecting stone or piece of timber for support; or oversailing courses of masonry.

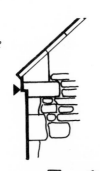

Crow-stepped
A term applied to gables, the coping of which rises in a series of steps.

Cruck
Pair of large curved timbers carrying ridge of building direct from ground, used throughout the middle ages.

Cupola
Strictly a dome but more usually describing a domed turret crowning a roof.

Diapering
In brickwork, burnt or glazed bricks set in a criss cross pattern.

Dormer Window
A vertical window on the slope of a roof and having a roof of its own.

Dutch Gable
(See Gable)

Eaves
The under part of a sloping roof overhanging a wall.

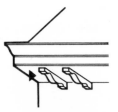

Entablature
Classical horizontal feature joining tops of columns or crowning wall face and comprising architrave, frieze and cornice.

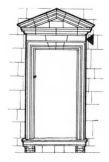

Fan Light
Small window, often semi-circular set in head of door opening.

Fascia
A plain or moulded board covering either the rafter feet at the eaves or the plate of a projecting upper storey.

Finial
A formal bunch of foliage or similar ornament at the top of a pinnacle, gable, canopy etc.

Gable
The wall at the end of a ridged roof, generally triangular, sometimes semi-circular.

Dutch-Gable – *a gable with multi-curved sides.*

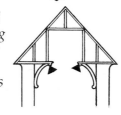

Hammer-beams
Horizontal brackets of a roof projecting at the wall plate level, and resembling the two ends of a tie beam with its middle post cut away, supported by braces or struts.

Hood-mould (or *moulded lintel*)
A projecting moulding on the face of a wall above an arch, doorway, or window. Sometimes it follows the form of an arch and sometimes it is square in outline.

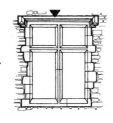

House Classifications
1. Hall and cellar type. Hall on first floor, rooms beneath generally vaulted.

2. H Type. Hall between projecting wings one containing living rooms, the other the offices. This is the usual form of a medieval house, employed with variations down to the seventeeth century.

3. L type. Hall and one wing. Generally small houses.

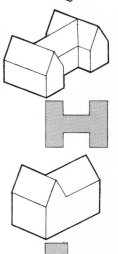

GLOSSARY

4. E type. Hall with two wings and a middle porch, usually sixteenth century and seventeenth century.

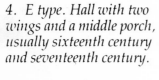

5. Half H type. A variation of the E type without the middle porch.

6. Courtyard type. House built round a court, sometimes only three ranges of building with or without an enclosing wall and gateway on the fourth side.

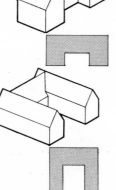

7. Central chimney type. Rectangular plan.

Jettied Storey
Projecting upper storey.

Jambs
The sides of an archway, doorway, fireplace, window or other openings.

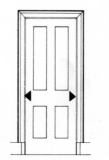

Key Stone
The middle stone in an arch.

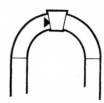

King-post
The middle vertical post in a roof truss, sometimes designed as a feature.

Kneeler
Stone at the foot of a gable.

Lancet
A long narrow window with a pointed head typical of the 13th century.

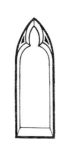

Lintel
The horizontal beam or stone bridging an opening.

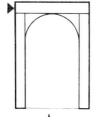

Louvre or Luffer
A lantern-like structure surmounting the roof of a hall or other building with openings for ventilation or the escape of smoke.

Mansard Roof
A form of roof having a break in the slope, the lower part being steeper than the upper.

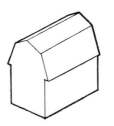

Mullion
An upright between two lights of a window.

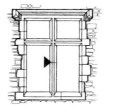

Modillions
Brackets under the cornice in Classical architecture.

Muntin
The intermediate uprights on the framing of a door, screen or panel, stopped by the rails.

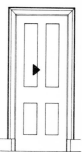

Oriel Window
A projecting bay window carried upon corbels or brackets.

Oversailing Courses
A number of brick or stone courses, each course projecting beyond the one below it.

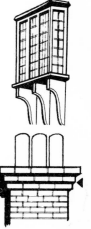

GLOSSARY

Pargetting
Ornamental plasterwork on the exterior of a building.

Pediment
A low pitched gable in Classical Architecture above a door, window or porch.

Pilaster
A shallow pier or column attached to a wall.

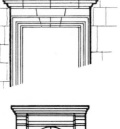

Plinth
The projecting base of a wall.

Queen Posts
A pair of vertical posts in a roof truss equidistant from the middle line.

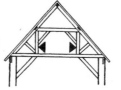

Quoin
The dressed stones or bricks at the angle of a building.

Riser
The vertical board of a step from tread to tread.

Shaft
The part of a chimney above the roof, in particular, the separate stalk terminating each flue. A small column.

Sash Window
A window having movable sash or sashes (usually sliding upwards) the sashes being the frame holding the glass.

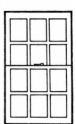

Soffit
The underside of a staircase, lintel, cornice, arch or canopy, the underside of a fixed beam or eaves.

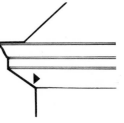

Spandrel

The space between the curve of an arch and the right angle formed by the jamb and the lintel. The space between a curved brace and a tie beam, and any similar triangular form.

Strut

A timber forming a sloping support to a beam.

Style

The vertical members of a frame into which are tenoned the ends of the rails or horizontal members.

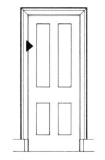

String

The sloping side piece enclosing or supporting the steps of a staircase.

Stud

The vertical post in a partition.

Tracery

The ornamental work in the head of a window, screen or panel formed by the curving and interlacing of bars of stone or wood, and grouped together usually over two or more lights or bays.

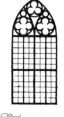

Transom

A horizontal bar of stone or wood across a window opening, doorway or panel.

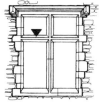

Truss

A number of timbers framed together to bridge a space or form a bracket, to be self supporting and to carry other timbers. In roof construction there is the King Post Truss and the Queen Post Truss for example.

Vaulting

An arched ceiling or roof of stone or brick, sometimes imitated in wood.

Wall Plate

A timber laid lengthwise on the wall to receive the rafters or studs.

LATE MEDIEVAL AND TUDOR

These houses were probably built in the second half of the 15th century.

Over the years the building has been modified; the very small original windows were replaced by casements in perhaps the 17th century, larger casements in perhaps the 18th century, a sash window in the early 19th century and then a pseudo Georgian bow in the 1960's.

The roof structure at the left hand end is said to be hipped and gabled. The two upper storeys project.

The small plastered cottage on the left has an eighteenth century front but it is in fact of the same period.

The terrace adjoins an ancient Guildhall built at about the same time.

Stoney Lane, Thaxted (c. 15th century)

16

LATE MEDIEVAL, TUDOR AND ELIZABETHAN

A good example of a half timbered house with herringbone brickwork between the studs, a form of construction often described as brick nogging.

There is elaborate wood carving below the oriel window, carved spandrels to the door and curved braces below the projecting storey.

This house was built in three stages, the left hand cross wing, a typical "priest's house" of the period, being the first. Notice the eaves carried straight across the centre hall on arched braces – a feature common in Kentish houses of this time (hence the term "Wealden" for these houses). The coved eaves are Elizabethan.

Monks Barn, Newport, Essex. (c. 15th century)

LATE MEDIEVAL AND TUDOR *(Stuart and Georgian alterations)*

A good example of an "H" plan house – a central hall with two storey cross wings on either side. The hall would have been open to the ridge originally and floored in later to provide an upstairs.

"H" is a basic plan that was used from the 13th to the 17th century.

This house was built in stages. The two wings are not of the same date – hence the differences in framing technique.

The windows are iron casements with mainly squared leaded lights typical of the 17th century.

The door is 18th century, a plain and simple door case.

The curved braces made from timbers carefully selected from local trees are of the type that has given rise to the old myth of "ships timbers". It's doubtful whether timber from ships was re used to any extent for inland houses.

The Old Vicarage, Newport, Essex. (c. 15th or 16th Century)

18

TUDOR AND ELIZABETHAN *(with later alterations)*

Another "H" plan house.

The jettied wing on the left is probably late 15th century and the rest of the house was built in Elizabeth's reign.

The early building was restored and modified in the 19th century. The elaborate barge boards and small wooden casement windows suggest the Regency period, a response to the fashion of the time.

The "Eyebrows" over the windows are probably Victorian.

The original clay peg tiles have recently been replaced with modern concrete tiles.

Tinden End, Wimbish (c. 15th or 16th century)

TUDOR *(Georgian, Victorian and Modern alterations)*

This building, now three cottages, was built as a yeoman's house in the early 16th century.

Notice the large chimney, an early window (top right hand), and later sliding casements upstairs.

The large sash downstairs would be early 19th century.

The left hand door head is original. The glazed door is modern.

The projecting storey running the entire length of the building is called a 'long jetty'.

Gold Street, Saffron Walden (c. 16th century)

20

TUDOR *(Victorian restoration)*

An example of a Tudor house which was much restored at the end of the last century. The front elevation was given a face lift so that the exposed timbers are now for ornamentation only. Notice how straight and equally spread they are.

The area below the original projecting upper storey has been enclosed with brick work enlarging the ground floor rooms.

Not really fake in spite of appearances, but much restored.

Priors Hall, Thaxted (c. 16th century)

LATE MEDIEVAL AND TUDOR

The general, although attractive disorder of this house tells us immediately that it's old – (planners would not accept it today).

Its very shape indicates a timber frame. Modern metal casements have replaced 18th century sash windows which in their turn would have replaced earlier windows.

The lower part of the building on the right appears to be an "L" plan hall house of the 15th or 16th century. The taller addition on the left was probably added in the 17th century.

Woodhams, Thaxted. (c. 15th or 16th century)

LATE MEDIEVAL OR TUDOR *(Stuart and later features)*

A good example of a "T" plan house, which like the "H" plan was a building shape used from the 13th to the 17th centuries. It is difficult to date except by expert examination of the timber details and joints.

Notice the jettied storey and the large chimney.

The lean to addition is a characteristic feature of small village houses.

The building still preserves the early hall house plan with a two storied cross wing. The dormer windows were probably added in the 17th century to give the main block another storey.

Littlebury (15th or 16th century)

TUDOR *(Stuart and Georgian)*

An interesting house.

Probably Tudor in origin, the overhanging (or jettied) storey suggests this period. There is elaborate pargetting along the concealed bressummer and the plaster dolphin was a 17th century inn sign. The plaster has been pitted with a pointed stick, a finish called scumbling.

Eighteenth century work includes the modillioned cornice (below the eaves) and the square bay windows with glazing bars.

The wing on the right with the shop front is late eighteenth or early nineteenth century and was originally residential. Inside there is an imposing hall with a very fine staircase.

Gold Street, Saffron Walden (c. 16th century)

ELIZABETHAN *(Georgian restoration)*

A very fine Elizabethan farmhouse with a large chimney with four diagonal shafts. The Gothic windows were put in in the late 18th century and the rather fine bay windows at the same time.
A solid looking door case of the same period completed the facelift.
The corner window is certainly unusual.

Radwinter (c. 16th century)

ELIZABETHAN

This Elizabethan manor house is of brick with a tiled roof.

The large brick buttresses each of three stages are carried up to the eaves.

The original windows are in stone with mullions (vertical) and transoms (horizontal).

The three very fine chimney stacks have octagonal brick shafts.

Brick became a fashionable building material for larger houses at this time.

Broadoaks, Wimbish (late 16th century)

TUDOR *(Georgian and Victorian)*

An interesting building. The middle section is the earliest part, sixteenth century, and the remainder probably seventeenth century. Notice the very fine doorway with the Venetian window over, added in the 18th century, the chimneys with diagonal shafts, the early sash windows upstairs and the later ones downstairs with their larger panes.

The building was given a brick front in the 19th century. The wing on the extreme left has a hipped gable. The flat roofed dormer is recent.

The Priory, Saffron Walden (c. 16th Century)

LATE STUART/WILLIAM & MARY

A fine building, late 17th century. Note the quoins, the sashes and the different shaped dormers, two with a triangular pediment and the centre one with a segmental pediment, a typical 17th century feature.

There is a very fine modillioned eaves cornice and an elaborate cupola, a fashionable feature in the latter half of the 17th century. This house was built in 1693 for a wealthy apothecary.

Bury St. Edmunds (c. 1693)

TUDOR *(Stuart or William and Mary restoration)*

A very fine house with elaborate pargetting and an outstanding hooded door.

The square leaded lights are 17th century.

The date above the door, 1692, refers to the pargetting and is the date that the earlier original timber framed building was given a facelift.

Such date marks usually refer to the plaster facade and seldom to the date of the original building.

Crown House, Newport (15th/16th century)

ELIZABETHAN *(Regency restoration)*

This original sixteenth century house was refaced in the late eighteenth or early nineteenth century. Note the elaborate bargeboards, and the bay windows, probably Regency.

The square casements are probably seventeenth century.

The top of the central chimney, just visible above the ridge, reveals three shafts.

High Street, Saffron Walden. (c. 16th century)

30

TUDOR *(Georgian restoration)*

A handsome house. Late Medieval frame and then a superb restoration in the 18th century.

A handsome door with columns based on the Doric Order, a pediment with modillions. The upper storey still projects as it did originally. Often the 18th century face lifters filled in the area below the projecting first floor to give a straight elevation and a larger ground floor area.

The roof is partly concealed by a parapet with a modillioned cornice. It originally had three gables which were cut back in the 18th century restoration.

The Market Cross, Thaxted. (c. 15th and 18th century)

ELIZABETHAN *(Georgian restoration)*

A very fine eighteenth century front on an earlier building. Large sash windows recessed in high arches with key stones. The parapet is pierced with balustrades above the modillioned cornice. There is a fine and massive chimney with diagonal shafts.

The picture below shows the back of the house and point "A" shows the side of the facade and gives an idea of how the front was added to the original to give it an eighteenth century face lift.

New House Farm, Radwinter (c. 16th century)

TUDOR *(Georgian restoration)*

The massive chimney with its diagonal shafts gives a good indication that this house belongs to an earlier period than the front suggests. The many features of this early Georgian facade include the rusticated brick pilasters to the door, the panelled parapet with a projecting cornice, and brick quoins. Bay windows became popular in the middle of the eighteenth century.

High Street, Saffron Walden (c. 16th century)

ELIZABETHAN *(Georgian restoration)*

A late eighteenth century front.

It has all the features of the period. Well proportioned sash windows with flat brick arches, an attractive door case with columns, architrave, frieze, cornice and pediment.

There is a plain brick parapet with a moulded eaves cornice.

A handsome house, probably of sixteenth century origin.

Church Street, Saffron Walden (c. 16th century)

WILLIAM & MARY *(Late Georgian restoration)*

A late eighteenth century front with beautifully balanced features, on an earlier frame.

An elegant door case, long sash windows. The dormers also have sashes.

There is a parapet with a projecting cornice and modillions and the roof is covered in heavy somewhat irregular Westmorland slates.

At the left hand corner are quoins.

Bury St. Edmunds (c. 1700, front c. 1800)

35

TUDOR *(Georgian and Modern restoration)*

This house is in fact very old, perhaps 15th century.
It was re-fronted in the 18th century and then again in
the 1930's when the balcony was added, bay windows
were taken out and replaced with the bow windows
you see. Note the eaves cornice and the 18th century
door cases.

Inside is a medieval hall with an unusual barrel vault
and with 16th century wall paintings.

The Priory, Thaxted (c. 15th century)

The Queen Anne and early Georgian period (1700 – 1760) is roughly in the middle of the period covered by these notes, 1450 – 1950, five hundred years, and midway we have the Queen Anne and Georgian houses.

The finest domestic houses date from here.

The houses of this period are of mainly simple designs, rectangular in shape and plan with sash windows and elegant front doors with hoods and fan lights.

It was an age of elegance in the domestic buildings of the period.

QUEEN ANNE

This house dates from 1718, for the year is recorded on the rainwater heads. A fine symmetrical facade of mellow brick. The windows, curved or segmental headed have keystones. An elegant front door with a segmental pediment, and the door pilasters are based on the Corinthian Order. Notice the parapet and the dormers which have alternate segmental and triangular pediments, a common device of the period. The dormers have casements and not sashes as in the other windows, in accordance with the fashion of the period.

As a matter of interest this particular house had Victorian bay windows inserted on the ground floor in the 19th century. In 1951 the front was rebuilt because of settlement and the bays were replaced with sashes and the building restored to original form.

Clarance House, Thaxted (c. 1718)

ELIZABETHAN *(Georgian alterations)*

A late eighteenth century front, on an earlier timber framed house.

Conventional sash windows with small panes and a plain door case.

The bow is a recent addition.

Note the end of the parapet which runs along the return frontage of this building and the front of the adjoining building.

Newbiggen Street, Thaxted. (c. 16th/17th century)

QUEEN ANNE *(Victorian restoration and extension)*

An interesting house. Although not immediately apparent the original part, the left hand end, is Queen Anne, early 18th century (see the second photograph which shows the opposite elevation.)

The house was obviously refronted in the mid nineteenth century and the right hand wing with its bay and eaves cornice was added.

An austere, straightforward but handsome house with sash windows and a plain door case.

High Street, Saffron Walden. (c. 1720)

REGENCY

The front is early nineteenth century. It has a very fine
front door with a beautiful fan light with very delicate
glazing bars.
To the ground floor there is a bay window; the first floor
vertical sash windows are long and match the overall
proportions of the design.
Above each sash is a keystone.
The parapet has a projecting cornice.

High Street,
Saffron Walden.
(c. 19th century)

40

EARLY GEORGIAN *(Regency/Victorian restoration)*

The front and the back of an 18th century house.

The rear elevation has original sash windows and is fairly intact.

The front has large Victorian sash windows to the ground floor, a fanlight of typical Regency design and the low pitched roof and the broad eaves of the Regency period.

The Manse, Thaxted. (c. 18th century)

GEORGIAN

A mid eighteenth century house with beautifully balanced features. A handsome door case, large bay windows below, small sash windows above and smaller dormer windows on top.

Dormers very often have casement windows even if the others are sash. Here are sashes in the dormers.

The building has a mansard roof with modillioned eaves cornice.

Pallets Farm, Newport. (c. 18th century)

GEORGIAN

An early nineteenth century front. Note the panelling between the bays, an interesting feature.

A handsome door case, casement dormers above the parapet and a mansard roof.

A fine archway, semi-circular and with a keystone, gave access for waggons to the maltings at the back.

Gold Street, Saffron Walden (c. 19th century)

ELIZABETHAN *(Georgian/Victorian restoration)*

A bold town house with steps and railings.

This is an eighteenth century front on a much earlier timber framed house. The bays were added in the 19th century.

The handsome door case with the classical features of columns and entablature with a triangular pediment was copied from one of the pattern books of the period.

High Street, Saffron Walden (c. 16th century)

REGENCY/EARLY VICTORIAN

A town house with a plastered front. Here is complete symmetry. The door case with fan light is set in a recessed arch above which is a keystone.

On either side of the door are bay windows to both ground and first floor. Note the thin and elegant glazing bars of this period (upstairs). Earlier glazing bars were much thicker.

At the angles of the facade are large quoins. The parapet is pierced with balustrades above the modillioned cornice, and is very similar to the parapet on the house page 17. (New House Farm, Radwinter).

High Street, Saffron Walden (c. late 18th century)

REGENCY

This Regency house with its sleek and austere lines was built about 1820. It is brick with a slated roof and contains no frills except the canopy running along the front verandah.

The sash windows to the upper storey and the long windows on either side of the front door, present a balanced and dignified design typical of the period.

Borough Lane, Saffron Walden (c. 1820)

REGENCY/EARLY VICTORIAN

An early nineteenth century terrace.

The grandeur and boldness of the eighteenth century is giving way in the left hand house to lighter, simpler features.

Notice the gable in the form of a pediment, the two storey bow windows and the bold front door with Doric columns.

The front elevation is stucco rendered. The pretty glazing bars in the left hand ground floor sash are worthy of note.

An elegant Regency terraced house suited to a country town.

Church Street, Saffron Walden (early 19th century)

REGENCY/EARLY VICTORIAN

This is a very handsome stucco fronted house.

A bold porch with plain Doric columns and entablature with graceful bows on either side.

A very low pitched roof with the broad eaves of the period.

Five sash windows to each of the two upper floors. A completely balanced design.

High Street, Saffron Walden (early 19th century)

EARLY VICTORIAN

An early nineteenth century facade with no frills, but very elegant. Serious and symmetrical with large sash windows, doorways on either side to balance, and very broad eaves.

As a matter of interest the door on the left belongs to the house next door and was incorporated in this building to give a balanced design.

Becket House, Thaxted (c. 1840)

LATE GEORGIAN

A late 18th or early 19th century cottage of brick and flint. The flints were obviously collected from the nearby fields.

The wide brickwork band beneath the first floor windows is patterned with flintwork shapes, and other brick courses frame flintwork panels.

Above the ground floor windows are segmental arches. The first floor windows are iron casements.

The builder obviously enjoyed his work and created a 'jolly' building.

Bolford Street, Thaxted. (c. 1800)

REGENCY

This is very unusual and perhaps unique. An early 19th century folly.

Brick and flint decorated with cinders and known as Cinder Hall. Built to look like a Tudor Castle with pierced battlement and Tudor style chimneys.

Cinder Hall, Saffron Walden (c. 1820)

REGENCY

This terrace of small dwellings was built, according to a date mark, in 1810.

Notice how each pair is stepped.

They are brick and have tiled roofs.

The windows are iron casements which were popular at this time, ironwork having come into its own in the second half of the eighteenth century.

The doorcases are straightforward, no frills, but well designed and attractive.

A neat and tidy terrace, perfectly balanced.

Gold Street, Saffron Walden. (1810)

REGENCY/EARLY VICTORIAN

These early 19th century estate cottages show the use of flint and pantiles, a frequent combination in country districts of East Anglia. They are well balanced and have deep dormer windows, this particular design is called trunk dormer.

Saxlingham, Norfolk (c. 1820)

EARLY VICTORIAN

An early nineteenth century house, actually built as a rectory.

On the right can be seen the earlier original cottage to which was added the principal house.

A handsome balanced building with long bay windows flanking the grand entrance with its Doric columns, and a low parapet with a plain cornice.

Saxlingham, Norfolk. (c. 1830)

VICTORIAN

This building is principally of flint, the stones having been collected from the surrounding fields.

Built in the mid nineteenth century its features include twin gables surmounted by finials (one missing).

Above the windows are moulded brick lintels, and the pretty iron window lights are notable.

The cluster of mock Tudor chimneys set diagonally indicate a fireplace in nearly every room.

Bridge End, Saffron Walden (c. 1860)

VICTORIAN

This forceful nineteenth century building is about 1860 and fairly described as Victorian Gothic.

It has a wealth of individual features. The doors and windows have lancet arches with elaborate embelishments.

There is a wide barge board to the gable, the roof tiles are shaped and the ridge tiles surmounted with ornamental crosses.

The clustered chimneys are copies of the Tudor period.

The external shape, rather than being designed for appearance is purely the result of enclosing a compact and convenient arrangement of rooms within.

High Street,
Saffron Walden. (c. 1860)

VICTORIAN

A mid Victorian Gothic house expressing the solidarity of the age. Built in 1864.

The roof lines are broken by gables of varying height and the ridges are crowned with openwork cresting.

Many smaller houses were built at this time with the same sort of features which include lancet windows, large square bays, varigated materials.

The architect, William Beck, also designed the house on page 56.

The Vineyard, Saffron Walden (c. 1860)

VICTORIAN

A delightful Victorian terrace of three town cottages.
Above the doors and windows are pointed arches and
the gables, small and large have elaborate barge boards.
Notice the course of ornamental brickwork.

Castle Street, Saffron Walden. (c. 1860)

VICTORIAN

This handsome block was built about 1850. It has lost the pure elegance of the eighteenth century but is still plain and straightforward and has not assumed the intricacy of later Victorian buildings. The shop front on the corner is a mid twentieth century modification.

Notice the modillioned cornice and the delicate frieze below.

The curved hip to the slate roof and the variety of windows on the top floor with slightly cambered arches, on the first floor semi-circular arches all contribute to the quality of the design.

An imposing building worthy of its prominent position in the market town High Street.

High Street, Saffron Walden (1850)

TUDOR/VICTORIAN *(Victorian restoration and extension)*

This house includes part of an original Tudor hall house with main block and cross wing. To this was added in the mid nineteenth century a rather massive extension of brick.

The long casement windows compliment the high roof line.

Wincelow Hall, Hempstead, Essex. (c. 17th and 19th century)

LATE VICTORIAN

Typical late Victorian houses similar to thousands built in every part of the country in the late 19th century. Strong features express the security of the age.

Note the pierced tiles forming open work cresting along the ridge and the ironwork galleries above the first floor bays.

Well built and solid.

Bury St. Edmunds. (late 19th century)

LATE VICTORIAN

An 'end of the nineteenth century' terrace following the lines of much earlier buildings.

The gables at each end project and they are faced with hanging tiles.

The dormers with triangular pediments match the gables.

Saffron Walden. (c. 1900)

MODERN *(1930's)*

Houses of this type, with windows in the roof were and still are often referred to as semi-bungalows or chalets.

They were popular between the wars. This one has an asbestos tiled roof, a roofing material which became popular for cheaper houses in this period.

The dormer windows are conspicuous for their size, mock Tudor exposed studs and barge boards.

Springhill Road, Saffron Walden (1930's)

MODERN *(1930's)*

This house is fairly typical of the "Between the Wars" period for the large detached house.

Rough edged elm boarding has been used to face the upper storey.

The metal casement windows were very popular in the nineteen thirties.

The hipped roof line follows the shapes of many old houses and is covered in cedar shingles, a form of roof covering never found on traditional Essex houses.

Bolford Street, Thaxted (1930's)

MODERN *(1930's)*

Semi-detached houses. These are typical of thousands in similar style which mushroomed all over England between the wars, 1920–1940. Many had bay windows with hanging tiles, and arched porches leading to the front door.

Their elevations were brick or, as in this picture, they were often pebble dash rendered, or roughcast.

Hipped roofs were often a feature.

In this picture the windows are wooden casements.

It was in this period that metal casements became popular.

Saffron Walden (1930's)

MODERN *(1940's)*

This pair of semi-detached houses was built immediately after the war, about 1946, and copies almost exactly the style between the wars.

Shortly after, in the 1950's semi-detached houses became generally plainer, the bays and recessed porches disappeared.

It was all a question of cost and the belated influence of functionalism.

Gibson Gardens, Saffron Walden (c. 1946)

MODERN *(1970's)*

A very modern house built to blend with a
Georgian house in the grounds of which it was built.
It emulates the 18th century designs, but its sash
windows are in aluminium and there are no glazing
bars.
The parapet screens the pitched roof.

Castle Hill, Saffron Walden (c. 1975)

MISCELLANEOUS DESIGNS

Modern houses of the sixties.
Unobstrusive buildings intended to blend with a variety of periods in a street.

Modern residential estate houses with plain lines.

Town houses with the principal accommodation on the first and second floors. Saffron Walden (c. 1960)

A fine Manor House. Queen Anne or perhaps William & Mary centre flanked on either side with late eighteenth century wings. Note the Venetian or Palladian window above the front door. The frame is probably Tudor.

Harston Manor, Cambridgeshire.

Eighteenth century bow windows in a Tudor house.

Stoke by Clare, Suffolk.

MISCELLANEOUS DESIGNS

*Straw thatched
hipped roof. Timber
framing with
herringbone brick
infill.
Hempstead, Essex.*

*Norfolk Reed thatched
roof.
Timber frame.
Eighteenth or early
nineteenth century
windows. Clare, Suffolk.*

*Early 18th century
elegance.
Saffron Walden,
Essex.*

*Late 18th century
flint cottages.
Saffron Walden,
Essex.*

MISCELLANEOUS DESIGNS

*Restored Tudor House
with modern bows.
Thaxted, Essex.*

Mid Victorian Flint Dutch gables. Near Saffron Walden.

Modern (1930) Estate Cottages with Dutch Gables. Norfolk.

A Hall House 15th century. The roof of the centre hall was often raised later to provide a first floor (see page 18). Saffron Walden, Essex.

MISCELLANEOUS DESIGNS

Early Victorian Town Houses.
Bury St. Edmunds.

Cobble stones.
Early 19th century.
Norfolk.

West Country stone.
Late 18th century.
Near Bude, Cornwall.

Mid nineteenth
century symmetry.
Radwinter, Essex.

MISCELLANEOUS DESIGNS

West Country Regency, 19th century Gothic windows.
Near Bude, Cornwall.

Genuine late 18th or early 19th century bow window.
Thaxted, Essex.

*Fine Tudor chimneys
of the 16th century
with four circular
shafts enriched with a
variety of design in
moulded brick and a
rectangular panelled
base.*
Clare, Suffolk.

*Similar chimneys on
what must have been
a house of the same
period, refronted or
almost rebuilt in the
eighteenth century.*
Clare, Suffolk.

MISCELLANEOUS MATERIALS

19th century estate
cottage. Mock Tudor
timbering and
chimneys.
Birdbrook, Essex.

Weatherboard or
clapboard elevations,
popular from the 18th
century.
Hempstead, Essex.

Tile Hanging.
Little Walden, Essex.

Acknowledgements
The author is greatly indebted to Miss Olive Cook,
Mr. Donald Purkiss R.I.B.A. and Mr. John Hunter
R.I.B.A. for their advice and interest, to Mrs. Delma
Barham for her assistance and to Mr. Richard
Jemmett for some of the photographs.